W9-BKY-213

My Sikh Year

Cath Senker

PowerKiDS press.

New York

Published in 2008 by The Rosen Publishing Group, Inc.
29 East 21st Street, New York, NY 10010

Copyright © 2008 Wayland/The Rosen Publishing Group, Inc.

First Edition

Picture Acknowledgments:
Art Directors & Trip Photo Library 14, 22 (H. Rogers); Chapel Studios 16 (Zul Mukhida); Circa Photo Library *Title page* (John Smith), 4 (B.J. Mistry), 9 (John Smith), 23 (Twin Studio), 26, 27 (John Smith); Prodeepta Das 8, 17; Paul Doyle *Cover*, 10, 15; Eye Ubiquitous 11 (Tim Page), 21 (David Cumming); Hodder Wayland Picture Library 20; Impact Photos 6 (Mohamed Ansar), 19 (David Harding); Nutshell Media 5 (Yiorgos Nikiteas); World Religions 7, 12 (Christine Osborne), 13 (Prem Kapoor), 18 (Gapper), 24, 25 (Christine Osborne).

Cover photograph: Carrying the Sikh flag in a procession for Vaisakhi.
Title page: A procession to celebrate Guru Nanak's Birthday.

Library of Congress Cataloging-in-Publication Data

Senker, Cath.
  My Sikh year / Cath Senker. -- 1st ed.
      p. cm. -- (A year of religious festivals)
  Includes bibliographical references and index.
ISBN-13: 978-1-4042-3733-9 (library binding)
  ISBN-10: 1-4042-3733-X (library binding)
  1. Fasts and feasts--Sikhism--Juvenile literature. I. Title.
  BL2018.37.S36 2007
  294.6'36--dc22
                          2006027558

Acknowledgments: The author would like to thank Amar Singh, Nina Manpreet Kaur Singh and Gurpreet Singh; Mohan Singh Nayyar, General Secretary of Gurdwara Sri Guru Singh Sabha, and Gurmukh Singh from the Sikh Missionary Society for all their help in the preparation of this book.

Manufactured in China

Contents

A Sikh life

Sikhs believe in one God. They follow the teachings of their Gurus. A Guru is a holy teacher. The Sikh holy book is the Guru Granth Sahib. It is read at festivals.

Sikhs believe all people are equal. They think that all religions should be respected, and that everyone should help other people.

These are the ten Sikh Gurus. They all helped to develop the Sikh religion.

This is Amar.
He has written a
diary about the
Sikh festivals.

Amar's diary

Wednesday, April 3

My name is Amar Singh. I'm
8 years old. I live with my dad,
mom, grandmother, and sister.
My sister is named Kiran Kaur
and she is 5. My family is from
India. I love playing soccer. At
school, I like games the best.
At home, I like playing on the
computer, drawing, and playing
with my cars. Because I'm a
Sikh, I don't cut my hair.

To show respect to God
and to their religion, Sikhs
do not cut their hair. Many
Sikh men wear a turban.

**This Sikh symbol is
called the Khanda.**

At the gurdwara

Sikhs meet at the gurdwara to pray and learn about their religion. When they arrive, they take off their shoes and cover their heads.

People pray in the worship hall. They sing hymns (this is called kirtan), and listen to a reading. Everyone has karah parshad—a special sweet. Then they enjoy a tasty shared meal, called langar.

In this gurdwara, you can see the Guru Granth Sahib covered by a cloth on the left. A woman is bowing to it to show respect.

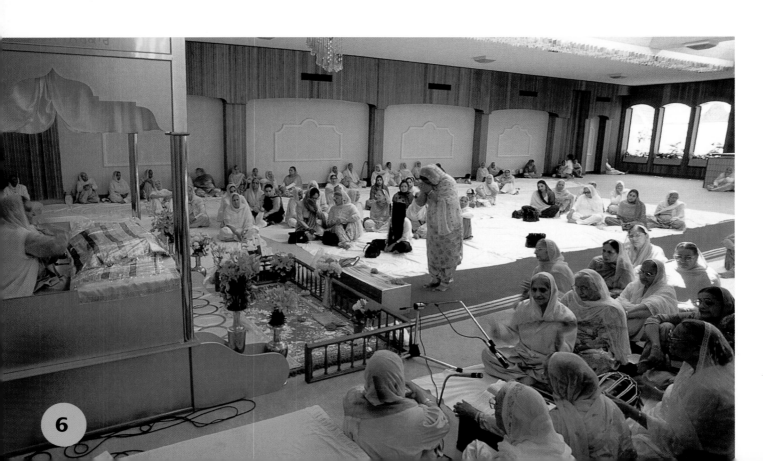

Sikhs take turns to cook and serve langar after worship.

Amar's diary

Sunday, April 7

Today, I went to the gurdwara with Dad, Mom, Kiran, and Grandma. When we went in, we bowed down to pay our respects to the Guru Granth Sahib. We all prayed together in the big hall. Then we ate langar. We had yogurt, rice, sweet rice, roti (bread), dhal (spiced lentils), and salad. My favorite food at the gurdwara is the dessert, the kheer.

For Sikhs, every day is a special day, so there is no particular day for worship. In Western countries, Sikhs usually go to the gurdwara on Sundays.

Sikh festivals

There are two kinds of Sikh festival: melas and gurpurbs. A mela is like a fair. It is a time for prayer and also a chance to have some fun!

The most important mela is Vaisakhi. The others are Divali and Hola Mohalla.

These bhangra dancers are celebrating Vaisakhi.

This procession in India is to celebrate Guru Nanak's Birthday.

Gurpurbs are festivals to honor Sikh Gurus. Sikhs celebrate on the anniversary of the Gurus' births and deaths. The most popular gurpurbs are Guru Nanak's Birthday and Guru Gobind Singh's Birthday.

Amar's diary
Thursday, April 11

My favorite festival is Vaisakhi, because we get lots of presents and sweets! We always do bhangra dancing at Vaisakhi. It's great fun. Sikhs have festivals to celebrate the birthdays of the Gurus. My favorite is Guru Gobind Singh's Birthday, when I play my drum at the gurdwara. The Gurus are important to us, because they teach us the right way to live.

Vaisakhi: New Yea

April

Vaisakhi is the most important mela. It marks the Sikh New Year. At Vaisakhi, Sikhs remember how their community, the Khalsa, first began.

On the festival day, people start by bathing. They pray quietly at home. Then they go to the gurdwara. They listen to a service about the Khalsa.

A procession in England to mark the Sikh New Year. You can see the Sikh symbol, the Khanda, on the flag.

SYMBOL OF SIKHISM

This boy is joining the Sikh community in a special ceremony. He sips Amrit five times. It is also sprinkled on his eyes and hair.

At Vaisakhi, Sikhs welcome new members to their community. Holy sugar water called Amrit is sprinkled on them. They promise to follow the Gurus' teachings.

Amar's diary
Saturday, April 13

Today it was Vaisakhi. We celebrated at home and in the gurdwara. At home, we prayed together and Grandma made lots of sweets for us. Then we gave each other presents. I got a new toy and some new pyjamas, and so did Kiran. We played with our new toys for a little while, and then we went to the gurdwara. At the gurdwara, we had some fruit and said our prayers.

Vaisakhi celebrations

Outside every gurdwara hangs the Sikh flag, the Nishan Sahib. At Vaisakhi, Sikhs take down the flagpole and flag. They wash the pole in yogurt to make it pure. They cover it with a fresh, new cloth and put on a new flag.

Everyone cheers as the clean flagpole is raised! The Nishan Sahib flies high again.

Groups of people perform bhangra dancing outside the gurdwara. There may be sports, arts, and music competitions.

The flagpole, with its new cloth and flag, is raised outside the gurdwara.

A display of Sikh martial arts at Vaisakhi. Martial arts are very important to Sikhs.

Amar's diary
Sunday, April 14

Yesterday at Vaisakhi, we watched the new flagpole being raised outside the gurdwara. Then competitions were held. I drew a picture, but I didn't win anything. Dad and I joined the bhangra dancing. I wore my kurtah pyjama, our traditional costume, but Dad wore jeans. Dad put Kiran on his shoulders while he was dancing, and Mom joined in, too.

Martyrdom of Guru Arjan

May/June

At this gurpurb, Sikhs remember Guru Arjan, their fifth Guru. He became a martyr for spreading the Sikh religion.

Guru Arjan was tortured. He was soaked in boiling water and had baking hot sand poured over him. He was not allowed to drink any water. Yet, he died calmly.

A picture of Guru Arjan. He put together the first Sikh holy book, the Adi Granth.

Sikhs in England give out free drinks to remember Guru Arjan.

In Guru Arjan's memory, Sikhs give away cool drinks to everyone. In India, it is hot at the time of this gurpurb, so the cool drinks are very welcome.

Amar's diary
Saturday, May 26

Today was the festival to remember Guru Arjan. At the gurdwara, people gave out kachi lassi—it's half milk and half water, with some sugar added. Some years there is fruit juice instead. At my school, there are Sikhs, Christians, Jews, Hindus, and Muslims. We talked about how everyone should be able to follow their own religion in peace.

15

The Guru Granth Sahib

August/September

Sikhs hold this festival to celebrate their holy book.

In 1708, Guru Gobind Singh, the tenth Guru, decided there would be no more human Gurus. The holy book, the Adi Granth, was to be the only guide for Sikhs. Its new name was the Guru Granth Sahib.

Men and women may read from the Guru Granth Sahib in the gurdwara.

A special fan called a chauri is waved over the Guru Granth Sahib to show respect.

Amar's diary
Monday, August 19

Today was the festival for celebrating our holy book, the Guru Granth Sahib. It's written in our Punjabi language. When it's written down, it's called Gurmukhi. I can't read it myself, but Grandma and Dad can. In the gurdwara, we look after the Guru Granth Sahib. We bow to it and pray to it. When we're not using the book, we cover it and put it in a special place.

At this festival, Sikhs worship in the gurdwara. They think about how they can follow the teachings of their holy book more closely.

Divali

October/November

Divali is a festival of light. Sikhs celebrate the time when their sixth Guru, Har Gobind, was freed from prison. When he arrived at the holy city of Amritsar, Sikhs lit candles and oil lamps to welcome him.

Since then, Sikhs have always celebrated with lights and fireworks. They light strings of lights, or clay lamps called divas.

These Sikhs in England are burning candles outside their gurdwara to celebrate Divali.

This man is handing out Indian sweets at Divali.

Amar's diary
Friday, October 19

Yesterday was the end of Divali. Mom and Dad gave me a football T-shirt, and Grandma gave Kiran and me lots of sweets. We knew it was a special day, because we usually only get one sweet a day. We went to the gurdwara and I lit a candle. Outside the gurdwara, there was a brilliant fireworks display. I watched it with my friends.

People dress in new clothes and give each other boxes of Indian sweets. There is music and dancing. In the evening, prayers are held at the gurdwara.

Guru Nanak's Birthday

November

This is a very important gurpurb.
Guru Nanak was born in 1469.
He started the Sikh religion.

In Sikh communities in the West,
there are fairs with stalls and games
to celebrate this day. In India,
there are lively processions.

Guru Nanak (second from the right) with two followers and two of his sons.

The Akhand Path reading finishes on the morning of the festival.

Amar's diary

Sunday, November 19

Yesterday was Guru Nanak's Birthday so we went to the gurdwara to pray. I listened to the end of the Akhand Path reading. Grandma was at the gurdwara for most of the day. I came home after two hours. We were told how Guru Nanak started our religion and what he taught the Sikhs. There was lots of food—and sweets, too. We could eat and drink as much as we wanted!

In the gurdwara, just before the festival begins, Sikhs take turns reading aloud from the Guru Granth Sahib. Reading the holy book all the way through is called Akhand Path. It takes about two days and two nights!

Martyrdom of Guru Tegh Bahadur

December

At this gurpurb, Sikhs remember the martyrdom of Guru Tegh Bahadur, their ninth Guru.

Over 300 years ago, the emperor of India tried to force all Indians to become Muslims. Guru Tegh Bahadur gave his own life to help to stop this.

Guru Tegh Bahadur believed people should be free to choose the religion they wanted to follow.

Young Sikhs take part in a procession for this gurpurb.

This festival is mainly celebrated in New Delhi, in India. There are big processions. Sikhs walk to the large gurdwara that was built where the Guru was killed.

Amar's diary
Thursday, December 20

Yesterday we remembered the martyrdom of Guru Tegh Bahadur. At the gurdwara, we found out that he gave his life to help other people. The granthi who led the service told us how brave the Guru was. We talked about being kind to other people and helping them. I always try to help my friends if they find something difficult in soccer that I can do easily.

Guru Gobind Singh's Birthday

December/January

This gurpurb is in memory of Guru Gobind Singh, the tenth Guru. He taught that there was only one God. He said that Sikhs should pray every day and help needy people.

These young Sikhs are learning to play the harmonium (front of picture) and the tabla.

Guru Gobind Singh was very good at writing music and poetry. At the gurdwara, Sikhs sing and play some of his hymns.

There may be games and sports competitions. People send each other greeting cards to mark the Guru's birthday.

The five Sikhs leading this procession stand for the first five members of the Sikh community.

Amar's diary
Saturday, January 5

Today, we celebrated Guru Gobind Singh's Birthday. Guru Gobind Singh told us always to wear the five Ks. These are: Kangha (comb), Kara (steel bangle), Kesh (uncut hair), Kachera (shorts), and Kirpan (sword). I'm still too young to carry a Kirpan. We performed some of the Guru's songs at the gurdwara. I played my dhol—a kind of drum. Dad taught me how to play.

Hola Mohalla

March

This festival celebrates springtime. In the past, the festival was a time when Sikhs trained for battle. Today, Sikhs still feel it is important for men and women to be strong and fit. They hold sports competitions and play games.

A display of martial arts at Hola Mohalla.

A man performs a show at Hola Mohalla in Anandpur, in India.

In the gurdwara, Sikhs read through the Guru Granth Sahib. They pray to keep healthy and strong.

Amar's diary
Sunday, March 31

My cousin Surinder has just come back from Hola Mohalla in India. She said there were mock battles, but no one really got hurt. Some people did clever tricks, like riding on a horse standing up! Then there were music and poetry competitions. They prayed, too, and on the last day there was a procession. Surinder said the langars at the festival were delicious.

Sikh calendar

April

Vaisakhi (3 days)
Sikhs remember how their community first began.

May/June

The martyrdom of Guru Arjan
(3 days) Sikhs remember their fifth Guru, Guru Arjan.

August/September

The Guru Granth Sahib (3 days)
The celebration of the Sikh holy book.

October/November

Divali (1 or 3 days)
The festival of light. Sikhs celebrate the time when their sixth Guru, Har Gobind, was freed from prison.

November

Guru Nanak's birthday (3 days)
At this festival, Sikhs remember Guru Nanak, who started the Sikh religion.

December

The martyrdom of Guru Tegh Bahadur (3 days)
Sikhs remember how their ninth Guru, Guru Tegh Bahadur, gave his life to defend others.

December/January

Guru Gobind Singh's birthday (3 days)
People sing and play hymns that were written by Guru Gobind Singh, the tenth Guru.

March

Hola Mohalla (3 days at Anandapur; 1 day everywhere else)
The Sikh spring festival, with sports and games.

Glossary

Adi Granth The first Sikh holy book.

Akhand Path The nonstop reading of the Guru Granth Sahib from beginning to end.

Amrit Holy water that is given during the Sikh baptism ceremony.

bhangra A dance from the Punjab in India.

dhol A drum with two sides, played with the fingers. It is often played in bhangra music and at weddings.

divas Lamps that use wicks made from twisted cotton dipped in melted butter. Many divas are lit at Divali.

granthi The person who takes care of the Guru Granth Sahib.

gurdwara The building where Sikhs go to meet and worship.

gurpurb A festival to remember the birth or death of a Guru.

Guru A holy teacher.

Guru Granth Sahib The Sikh holy book. It is seen as a living Guru.

honor To show admiration and respect for a person.

karah parshad A sweet made from semolina, butter, and sugar. It is blessed and then everyone is given some.

Khalsa The Sikh community.

kheer An Indian dessert made from rice, milk, and sugar.

kirtan Singing hymns from the Guru Granth Sahib.

kurtah pyjama A long cotton shirt and cotton pants. This is a traditional Sikh costume.

langar The free food people eat at the gurdwara.

martial arts Sports that use fighting skills, such as judo and karate.

martyr A person who is killed because of their religion.

martyrdom The death of a person because of their religion.

mela A word that means 'fair'. It is used to describe festivals that are not gurpurbs.

Nishan Sahib The Sikh flag that flies outside the gurdwara.

reading A part of the Guru Granth Sahib or another Sikh religious book. It is read out to people in the gurdwara.

tabla A pair of small drums.

For Further Reading

Books to Read

Buddhists, Hindus and Sikhs in America (Religion in American Life) by Gurinder Singha Mann (Oxford University Press, USA, 2002)

Sikhism (World Religions) by Joy Barrow (Walrus Books, 2005)

The Kids Book of World Religions by Jennifer Glossop (Kids Can Press, 2003)

The Best Feasts and Festivals from Many Lands (Kids Around the World) by Lynda Jones (Jossey-Bass, 1999)

World Religions (History Detectives) by Simon Adams (Southwater, 2004)

Places to Visit

Asian Art Museum
200 Larkin Street
San Francisco, CA 94102
Tel: 415.581.3500
www.asianart.org/

Los Angeles County Museum of
Art 5905 Wilshire Boulevard
Los Angeles, CA 90036
Tel: 323-857-6000
www.lacma.org

Due to the changing nature of Internet links, Powerkids Press has developed an online list of Web sites related to the subject of this book. This site is updated regularly. Please use this link to access the list:
www.powerkidslinks.com/ayrf/sikh

The author

Cath Senker is an experienced writer and editor of children's information books.

Index